THE MARRIAGE STORY ™

A TIMELESS TALE ABOUT STAYING IN LOVE FOR LIFE

DENNIS EDWARD GREEN

Boulevard Press
www.BoulevardPress.com

THE MARRIAGE STORY
© Copyright 2011, Dennis Edward Green, All Rights Reserved.

Printed in the United States of America. No part of this book may be reproduced in any form without permission in writing from the author, except in the case of brief quotations embodied in critical articles or reviews.

Boulevard Press books may be purchased for educational, business, or sales promotion use. For information, please send email to Sales@BoulevardPress.com

Library Of Congress Control Number 2011911416

ISBN 978-0-9832411-3-3

First Edition

Boulevard Press
www.BoulevardPress.com

With Love And Appreciation

This story poem was originally written longhand in a restaurant one afternoon in 1975, but never published, until 2011. I have added a few pages to it since writing the original story.

At the time I wrote it, I was feeling like a failure. I guess the poem was an expression of both my defeat and my hope for the future. Or maybe it was an expression of how easy it is to get lost when you don't know what really matters.

This book is dedicated to Mary Lou, my wife of 33 years, who has shown me what is important in life. Thank you for never letting a day go by without making me feel loved and loving.

<blockquote>There is no point in being me
without you.</blockquote>

Thank you

I read this story to our son Dennis, and our daughter-in-law Kathleen, on the eve of their wedding in 2001. The book may never have seen the light of day if not for their encouragement.

The Marriage Story

*We all share a
common struggle to decide
what is most important
in our lives.
When we are lucky enough
to love someone,
and to be loved in return,
we find the answer.*

They held each other
on a moonlit night,
young lovers taking time
to be alone.

Their smiles were soft,
words were hardly spoken.
Their loving hearts
set a tender tone.

She loved how he held her
so carefully close.
He was warm and gentle,
yet so strong.

He whispered that he loved her,
and that filled her with joy.
She had waited to hear it
for so long.

"I love you more than life,"
he whispered.
"You are all I ever wanted,"
he extolled.

"My love will last forever
if you'll have me," he went on.
Yet, she wondered, will he love me
when I'm old.

Sensing her concern,
he quickly assured her,
"My feelings
are strong and true."

"I believe you," she said.
"And no matter what happens,
I will never love anyone,
but you."

So they pledged their love
in an old stone church.
He wore black.
She dressed purely in white.

They shared their bed
under a star-laden sky,
and two became one
that first night.

They spent the next year
learning to share,
addressing each other's
every need.

They were fitted to love
like a hand in a glove,
quite perfectly suited
indeed.

She said, "I promise to share all my thoughts with you. But you must do the same with me.

If we talk to each other, we will stay in love forever, even if we occasionally disagree."

*The days flew by
and their love kept growing,
even more than either
could have guessed.*

*They talked and touched
on their hopes and fears,
and their love passed
each challenging test.*

As time flowed on
they talked about the future,
thinking and planning
a perfect life.

He worked very hard
to be a devoted husband.
She strived to be
a perfect wife.

They sacrificed much
to build their dream.
They bought a house and invested
to get ahead.

"If we work like our parents
and do what's expected,
no doubt we'll be happy,"
they said.

*They needed things,
so they worked a little harder.
They agreed it was important
to grow.*

*But they worked so much,
commuting and such,
that they spent all their time
on the go.*

They had everything
lovers need to be happy.
But, they thought that they
needed more.

They believed the old sayings,
"You only go around once."
And, "Money is how you
keep score."

The ensuing years
fulfilled all their wishes.
He got promotions, and she got
a boy.

She took excellent care
of both her fine men.
He worked harder to secure
their joy.

Together they strived to be
thoughtful parents,
committed to enriching
a third life.

They smothered their child
with undying affection,
being more than a husband
and a wife.

Before long they decided
their son might be lonely.
"He should have a sister,"
they agreed.

So they tried right away,
every 25th day,
until their daughter was carefully
conceived.

Eventually it turned out
just as they had planned.
Their second was born a healthy
girl.

She had big happy eyes.
She hardly ever cried,
and she had hair with a natural
curl.

In time they concluded
their house was too small.
They definitely needed more
space.

So they decided to move
out to the suburbs,
and buy a much bigger
place.

But along with their move
came new demands,
a second car just to go to
the store.

Then they built a pool
and a fence for the dog,
so of course they had to
earn more.

She stayed home with the kids.
He worked more hours,
so they could have what they
always dreamed.

They thought they'd be fine
if he worked overtime,
but there was never enough,
or so it seemed.

But, as they scraped and struggled
to capture true bliss,
minor changes began to
take place.

They came home from work
so terribly tired,
and she rarely wore a smile
on her face.

*Something's not right
they separately thought,
but rarely shared how they were
feeling.*

*She wondered when
they might make love again,
and feared she was no longer
appealing.*

They didn't laugh much anymore
and very rarely went out.
It was clear they were going
through a change.

He buried his feelings
deep down inside.
She told friends he was acting
quite strange.

"It's just my workload.
Don't worry about me,"
he told her one night
before bed.

"When I get that promotion,
the kids can have braces,
and everything will be perfect,"
he said.

*But as their lives continued,
they drifted apart.
If one said black, the other
thought white.*

*Her energies focused
entirely on the children.
They stopped touching and
started to fight.*

Their interests changed, too,
as the years went by.
She went shopping and
he came home late.

"All you do is spend money,"
he complained.
She snapped back,
"You need to lose weight."

He traveled for work
more than ever these days,
and rarely called home
on the phone.

She no longer waited up
to take his call,
but wondered if he was
sleeping alone.

She didn't understand
what was happening to them.
Her friends advised her
to be strong.

"I want to blame it
on something," she cried.
"But I don't even know
what is wrong."

"It is just a stage,"
friends tried to assure her.
"All couples have troubles
some day."

She wanted to blame
their problems on him,
but worried she had made things
this way.

He and his friends never
discussed their problems.
Failure doesn't look good
on a man.

"The family's all fine,"
was his usual line.
"Life is working according
to plan."

But he knew in his heart,
he was falling apart.
His job wasn't working out
so well.

He was racing with time,
passing his prime.
And his gray was beginning
to tell.

She went about her day
hoping things would change,
praying he'd open up so she
would know.

She brought up the idea of
seeing a counselor,
but he was never ready
to go.

He said, "There's no point
in whining about life.
Complaining to a stranger
is absurd.

We don't need a shrink
to tell us how to think."
After that she never mentioned
the word.

The years rolled on,
and nothing really changed.
They adapted to each other
as best they could.

Their children grew up
and went on their own,
and she looked back to when
life seemed so good.

*She wondered if they'd ever feel
passionate again.
But that seemed sadly
in doubt.*

*If there was only a way
to get back to the day
when they knew what love
was about.*

But that was much harder than
she had imagined.
It's a very long way back
to then.

Still, she listened to a friend
who said, "Don't lose hope.
It is possible to find love
again."

*On weekends he fished,
she worked in her garden,
and they talked to the kids
on the phone.*

*She prepared the meals,
and he took out the garbage.
But it was like they were
living alone.*

The years moved on.
They were civil to each other,
filling time with
menial stuff.

Then, without warning, he was
laid off from work,
and they realized they hadn't
saved enough.

*She remembered promises they
had made long ago,
and how they had let love
slip away.*

*More than ever now,
they needed one another,
but couldn't find the words
to say.*

Then one afternoon,
out of character for him,
he asked her to join him
for a walk.

She wanted to know where
he wanted to go.
He said he just needed
to talk.

She was still half in shock
as they left the house,
heading out through their open
gate.

He talked as they strolled.
She listened intently.
"I was thinking about our first
date."

"The first time I saw you
I felt struck by lightning.
I told my brother you were a
perfect ten."

"And I told my girlfriend
you were the exception," she said,
"to the rule that there are no
perfect men."

She went on talking,
"We had fun back then."
And she reached out and took
his hand.

He said, "Yes, we did,
thanks mostly to you.
You're the only true success
I ever planned."

*"If that's how you feel,
then what's happened to us?
I don't feel like a roaring
success."*

*He paused on the path
and turned to face her.
"I know, I've made our lives
a mess."*

She said, "I understand,
but I'll take my share of blame."
He said nothing.
His eyes searched the ground.

She asked, "Do you sometimes feel
that you got a raw deal?"
He shook his head,
but still made no sound.

They strolled and found a swing
suspended from a tree.
They sat down and he proceeded
to hold her.

They sat there in silence,
as she nestled in his arms.
"You're the deal of a lifetime,"
he told her.

He said, "I've been depressed
for a very long time.
That's not exactly a news flash,
I know.

For years I've been feeling
like I was becoming invisible,
a nobody with nothing
to show."

"I know it must be hard
to understand what I'm saying,
after all that I've put you
through."

She said, "I've been worried
out of my mind,
but I didn't know what
to do."

> "I didn't know either.
> I kept having this dream
> that I was trapped in a room
> with no door.
>
> Everything I ever owned
> was stacked from floor to ceiling,
> and yet I was desperately
> poor."

"Does that mean that you felt
trapped in our marriage,
but you couldn't
see a way out?"

He touched her cheek,
then he held her hand.
"No, that's not what the dream
was about."

"I didn't understand anything until yesterday afternoon. My friend Marcus called me with the answer.

We hadn't talked in years, so I was happy to hear his voice, until he said he just discovered he had cancer."

*"I was completely devastated.
I didn't know what to say.
I couldn't believe it was
true.*

*Then he asked me,
if I had three months to live,
what would I choose
to do?"*

"*My thoughts leaped to you
and the first time we kissed
on that beach under a midnight
moon.*

*And I recalled you in the garden
behind our first house,
planting tomatoes and singing
off-tune.*"

"I pictured us all together,
the kids in our arms,
at a time when everything
felt right.

Then I saw that room again,
the one with no door,
only now the space was open
and bright."

*"A doorway appeared
and you were standing there,
reaching your hand out
to me.*

*I stepped over the threshold,
took you in my arms,
and suddenly I felt completely
free."*

"That's when I told Marcus
if I had three months to live,
I would spend every moment with
my wife.

I told him whatever happened
from this day on,
she would be all that mattered, in
my life."

"Then he said something
that shook me to the core.
He said, 'I have no one to love
. . .at this time.'

The way it came out
made me profoundly sad.
It was like he was confessing
to a crime."

"When I got off the phone,
I felt selfish and vain
telling Marcus what he needed
to do.

I could drop dead tomorrow,
yet here I am,
squandering time I could spend
loving you."

*"I have done my share
of wasting time," she said.
"After the kids moved away
I knew...*

*I was only treading water,
doing things that didn't matter,
instead of being a true partner
for you."*

They sat there for hours
talking back and forth,
sharing regrets to the rhythm
of the swing.

And as the afternoon light
faded softly into night,
he took her hand and kissed
her wedding ring.

"I love you more than life,"
he whispered.
"You are all that ever mattered,"
he extolled.

"My love will last forever
if you'll have me once again."
She laughed, "Forever's not that long
when we're this old."

He laughed along with her.
"Then I can't waste a moment.
I have years of repairing
to do."

She said, "Let's go back to when
we only needed each other."
He said, "I'll go anywhere
with you."

They rocked in the swing
and gazed into the distance,
watching moonlight dance
upon the lake.

They talked about how
they could stay in love forever,
and they vowed to do whatever
it would take.

*They remained there awhile
swaying in the breeze,
bathing in the moon's
healing light.*

*With their minds now at peace
and their spirits joined once more,
old lovers fell in love again
that night.*

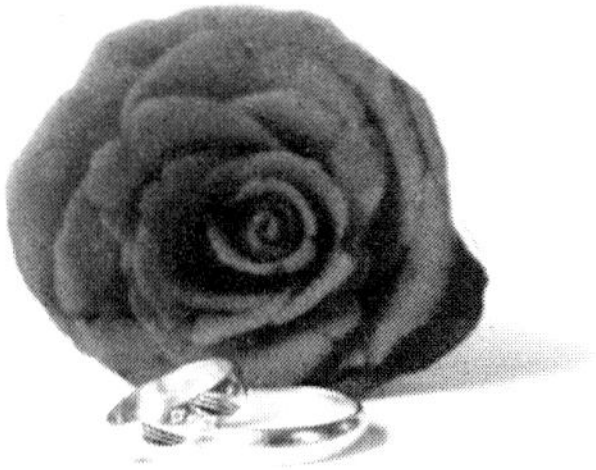

Scan this QR code to go directly to the
author's website
http://www.DennisAndMaryLou.com